JAVA FOR BEGINNERS

A Simple Start To Java Programming (Written By A Software Engineer)

Scott Sanderson

Table of Contents

Introduction	3
Java - Basic Syntax	7
Objects and Classes	15
Basic Data Types	27
Variable Types	34
Operators in Java	42
Loops in Java	52
Decision Making	62
Strings in Java	72
Arrays	81
Regular Expressions	87
Methods	97
File Handling	111
Exception Handling	123
Interfaces and Packages	131
Java Applets	135

Other Scott Sanderson Books

BONUS

Copyright 2014 by Globalized Healing, LLC - All rights reserved.

Introduction

Java, the programming language, was introduced by Sun Microsystems. This work was initiated by James Gosling and the final version of Java was released in the year 1995. However, initially Java was released as a component of the core Sun Microsystem platform for Java called J2SE or Java 1.0. The latest release of Java or J2SE is Java Standard Version 6.

The rising popularity of Java, as a programming platform and language has led to the development of several tools and configurations, which are made keeping Java in mind. For instance, the J2ME and J2EE are two such configurations. The latest versions of Java are called Java SE and Java EE or Java ME instead of J2SE, J2EE and J2ME. The biggest advantage of using the Java platform is the fact that it allows you to run your code at any machine. So, you just need to write your code once and expect it to run everywhere.

As far as the features of Java are concerned, they are as follows:

- Object Oriented
  In Java, everything is an object. Java can be effectively stretched out and extended to unimaginable dimensions since it is focused around the Object model.
- Independent of the platform
  Dissimilar to numerous other programming dialects including C and C++, when Java is aggregated, it is not converted into a form, which is particular to any machine. Instead, it is converted into a machine-independent byte code. This byte

code is conveyed over the web and deciphered by Virtual Machines or JVM on whichever stage it is generally run.

- Simple

  Java is intended to be not difficult to learn. In the event that you comprehend the essential idea of OOP, Java would not be difficult to ace.

- Secure

  With Java's security framework, it empowers to create frameworks, which are free of viruses and tampering. Public-key encryption is used as the core authentication strategy.

- Independent of Machine Architecture

  Java compiler produces an object file format, which is independent of the architecture of the machine. The assembled code can be executed on numerous processors, with the single requirement that they must all have Java runtime framework.

- Portability

  The fact that Java code is machine and platform independent makes it extremely compact. Compiler in Java is composed in ANSI C with a clean conveyability limit, which is a POSIX subset.

- Robustness

  Java tries to kill circumstances, which can lead to potential system failures, by stressing chiefly on runtime checking and compile time checking.

- Support for Multithreaded Applications

  With Java's multithreaded feature, it is conceivable to compose programs that can do numerous assignments at the same time.

This configuration gimmick permits designers to build easily running intelligent applications.

- Interpreted Code

  Java byte code is interpreted on the fly to local machine. The advancement methodology is more quick and expository since the interfacing is an incremental and lightweight process.

- High Performance

  With the utilization of Just-In-Time compilers, Java enhances the performance of the system.

- Distributed

  Java is intended for the conveyed environment of the web.

- Dynamic

  Java is thought to be more dynamic than C or C++ since it is intended to adjust to an advancing environment. Java projects can convey broad measure of run-time data that can be utilized to check for accesses and respond to the same on run-time.

History of Java

James Gosling started working on the Java programming language in June 1991 for utilization in one of his numerous set-top box ventures. The programming language, at first, was called Oak. This name was kept after an oak tree that remained outside Gosling's office. This name was changed to the name Green and later renamed as Java, from a list of words, randomly picked from the dictionary.

Sun discharged the first open usage as Java 1.0 in 1995. It guaranteed Write Once, Run Anywhere (WORA), giving no-expense run-times on prominent stages. On 13 November 2006, Sun discharged much of Java as free and open source under the terms of the GNU General

Public License (GPL). On 8 May 2007, Sun completed the procedure, making the greater part of Java's center code free and open-source, beside a little parcel of code to which Sun did not hold the copyright.

Pre-requisites

In order to run and experiment with the examples given in this book, you shall require a Pentium 200-Mhz machine with at least 64 MB of RAM. You additionally will require the accompanying programming platforms:

- Microsoft Notepad or Any Word Processor
- Java JDK 5
- Linux 7.1 or Windows XP or higher Operating Systems

Java - Basic Syntax

A basic Java program can be broken down into several constructs and elements. Typically, it can be characterized as a collection of objects, which communicate with each other by calling each other's routines. The basic definitions of objects and classes are given below:

- Class

  A class can be described as a blueprint that portrays the practices/expresses all the behaviors and states of its objects.

- Object

  Objects are characterized by two components namely, methods and attributes or variables. For instance, if you consider the example of a puppy, then it has the following attributes or states: name, color and breed. In addition, it also has the following behaviours, which include woofing, wagging and consuming. Any object is nothing but an instance of a class.

- Instance Variables

  Each object has its set of variables. An object's state is made by the qualities alloted to these variables during program execution.

- Methods

  A method is the definition of a method. Moreover, a class can contain numerous methods. It is in these methods that behaviours like where the rationales are composed, information is controlled and all the activities are executed.

First Java Program:

In order to start with basic basic Java programming, let us look at the standard Hello World program.

```
public class MyFirstJavaProgram {
    public static void main(String []args) {
    System.out.println("Say Hello World To The World!");
    }
}
```

As you can see, the program uses a single line of code in the main() function, which prints the statement 'Hello World!'. However, before that can be done, let us look at the steps that you must follow in your quest to execute the file.

- Open any text editor and paste this code in that file.
- Save the file with a .java extension. For example, you can save the file as Sample.java.
- The next step is to to open the command prompt of the system and relocate its reference to the directory in which the file is saved. For instance, if you have saved the file in C:\, then you must take the prompt to the same directory.
- In order to compile the code, you must type the following:
  javac Sample.java
- If there are no errors, you will automatically be taken to the next line. You can now execute the code using the following command:
  java Sample.java
- You should be able to see the following output on the screen.
  Say Hello World To The World!

Basic Syntax

About Java programs, it is paramount to remember the accompanying points.

- Class Names –
  For all class names, the first letter ought to be in Upper Case. On the off chance that few words are utilized to structure a name of the class, every internal word's first letter ought to be in Upper Case. For example, a standard class name is as follows:
  class Sampleclass
- Case Sensitivity - Java is case sensitive, which implies that the identifier Hi and hi would have distinctive importance in Java.
- Method Names - All system names ought to begin with a Lower Case letter. In the event that few words are utilized to structure the name of the method, then every internal word's first letter ought to be in Upper Case. An example of this convention is follows:
  public void mysamplemethod ()
- Filename –
  The name of the system record ought to precisely match the class name. At the point when you are saving the file, you ought to save it utilizing the class name. Remember Java is case touchy and affix ".java" to the end of the name. If the document name and the class name don't match your system won't assemble. Consider the example of a class name Sample. In this case, you must name the file as sample.java.

- public static void main(string args[])

  Java system handling begins from the main() function, which is a required piece of each Java program.

Java Identifiers

All Java components require names. Names utilized for classes, variables and strategies are called identifiers. In Java, there are a few focuses to recall about identifiers. They are as per the following standard:

- All identifiers ought to start with a letter (beginning to end or a to z), underscore (_) or special character ($).
- After the first character, identifiers can have any mix of characters.
- You cannot use a keyword as an identifier.
- Most significantly, identifiers are case sensitive. So, Sample is not same as sample.
- Examples of identifiers include $salary, age, __1_value and _value.
- Examples of illicit identifiers include −compensation and 123abc.

Java Modifiers

Like is the case with any programming language, it is conceivable to alter classes and systems by utilizing modifiers. There are two classifications of modifiers:

- Access Modifiers: public, default, protected and private

- Non-access Modifiers: strictfp, final and abstract

We will be researching more insights about modifiers in the following chapters.

Java Variables

Several types of variables are supported by Java. These types of variables include:

- Instance Variables (Non-static variables)
- Class Variables (Static Variables)
- Local Variables

Java Arrays

Arrays are contiguous memory locations that store different variables of the same sort. On the other hand, an array itself is an article on the memory. We will research how to proclaim, develop and instate these in the chapters to follow.

Java Enums

Enums were introduced as part of the Java package in java 5.0. Enums limit a variable to have one of just a couple of predefined qualities. The qualities in this identified list are called enums. With the utilization of enums it is conceivable to diminish the quantity of bugs in your code. Case in point, in the event that we consider an application for a cafe, it would be conceivable to limit the mug size to extra large, large, medium and small. This would verify that it would not permit anybody to request any size other than the sizes mentioned in the menu or application listing.

Please note that enums can be pronounced as their own or inside a class. However, routines, variables, constructors can be created inside the body of enums as well.

Java Keywords:

Kcywords or reserved words in Java are shown in thc table below. As a rule, these words cannot be used as names for variables or constants.

- assert
- abstract
- break
- boolean
- case
- byte
- char
- catch
- const
- class
- default
- continue
- double
- do
- enum
- else
- final
- extends
- float
- finally
- goto
- for
- implements
- if
- instanceof
- import
- int
- long
- interface
- new

- native
- private
- package
- protected
- return
- public
- static
- short
- super
- strictfp

- synchronized
- switch
- throw
- this
- transient
- throws
- while
- try
- volatile
- void

Comments in Java

Just as in the case of C++ and C, Java supports two types of comments namely, single line comments and multi-line comments. The syntax for these types of comments are as follows:

Single line comment:

//<comment>

Multiple line comment:

/*<comment>*/

All characters that exist in the comments region are simply ignored by the Java compiler.

Using Blank Lines:

Any line that is only composed of whitespace characters or comments is considered a blank line. These lines are just ignored by the compiler and are not included in the executable.

Inheritance:

Java supports inheritance. In other words, it is possible to derive one class from another class in this programming language. For instance, if you need to create a new class, which is an extension of an existing class, then you can simply derive this new class from an existing class. This allows the new class to access the elements already implemented in the existing class. In this case, the new class is called the derived class and the existing class is referred to as the super class.

Interfaces:

As mentioned previously, Java is all about interaction between objects. The manner in which different objects communicate with each other is defined in what is called an 'interface.' Moreover, interfaces are also an important aspect of the inheritance feature of java. As part of an interface, the methods that can be used by a derived or sub-class are declared. However, all the methods declared as usable for the subclass must be implemented in the subclass.

Objects and Classes

Java is an Object-Oriented programming language. As an issue that has the Object Oriented peculiarity, Java underpins the accompanying essential ideas:

- Inheritance
- Polymorphism
- Abstraction
- Encapsulation
- Objects
- Message Parsing
- Classes
- Method
- Instance

In this part, we will investigate the concepts of Classes and Objects.

- Class - A class can be described as an blueprint that declares and defines the attributes and methods that its objects will implement and use.
- Object - Objects are simple real world entities that possess a state and its characteritic behaviour.

For example, if you consider a real world entity, a labrador dog, then this dog is an object. However, it belong to the class of dogs. Therefore, the associated class is Dog.

Objects in Java

Let us now look profoundly into what are objects. In the event that we consider this present reality, we can discover numerous entities around us, Cars, Humans, Dogs and several other. N fact, any real world entity can be modelled as an object. The one common thing between all these entities is the fact that they contain states and behaviours. On the off chance that we consider a dog, then its state is - breed, name and color. However, its behaviour includes eating habits and other characteristics like running and barking.

Classes in Java

A class is a blue print from which individual objects are made. A specimen of a class is given underneath:

open class Dogs {

String breed;

String shade;

int age;

void eating (){ }

void barking (){ }

}

A class can contain any of the accompanying variable sorts.

- Local variables

Variables that are declared and used inside routines, constructors or pieces of code are called local variables. The variable will be proclaimed and instated inside the method or scope and the variable will be destroyed when the execution of a method terminates.

- Instance variables

  Instance variables are variables inside a class yet outside any system. These variables are instantiated when the class is stacked. These variables can be gotten to from inside any technique, constructor or squares of that specific class.

- Class variables

  Class variables will be variables, which are declared within a class, outside any system, with the static word before them.

A class can have any number of routines to get to the estimation of different sorts of methods. In the above illustration, eating() and barking() are the used methods. Underneath specified are a percentage of the vital subjects that need to be examined when researching classes of the Java Language.

Constructors

At the point when talking about classes, a standout amongst the most vital sub theme would be constructors. Each class has a constructor. In the event that we don't unequivocally compose a constructor for a class, the Java compiler manufactures a default constructor for that class. Each time an object is made, no less than one constructor will be summoned.

The fundamental principle of constructors is that they ought to have the same name as the class. A class can have more than one constructor and depending on the parameters given and return type expected, the matching constructor is called. A sample implementation for this type of a method is given below:

public class Puppies{

public Puppies(){

}

public Puppies(string puppyname){

}

The above class has two constructors. One of the constructors requires no parameters. However, the other constructor requires a string equivalent to the name of the puppy. Java additionally upholds Singleton Classes where you would have the capacity to make one and only object of a class.

Making Objects

As specified previously, a class gives the outlines to object creation. So, fundamentally an object is made from a class. In Java, the new essential word is utilized to make new objects.

There are three steps involved in the creation of any object. These steps are illustrated below:

- Declaration: A variable assertion with a variable name and object type.
- Instantiation: The "new" word is utilized to make the object of an already declared class.
- Initialization: The "new" word is trailed by a call to a constructor. This call instantiates the class and creates an object of the same, as a result.

Sample implementation is given below for better understanding of the concept.

public class Puppies{

public Puppies(string name){

    System.out.println("Passed Name of the puppy is:" + name);

}

public static void main(string []args){

    Puppies samplepuppy = new Puppies("jimmy");

}

On the off chance that we compile and run the above project, then it would deliver the accompanying result:

Passed Name of the puppy is: jimmy

Getting to Instance Variables and Methods:

Variables and methods are gotten to by means of made objects of classes. To get to a variable, the qualified way ought to be the following:

The following statement creates an object.

Newobject = new Constructormethod();

The following statements can be used to access the variable and method associated with the object.

Newobject.variablesname;

Newobject.methodsname();

A sample implementation of this concept is given below:

public class Dog{

int dogAge;

public dogAge(String dogname){

    System.out.println("Dog Name Passed is :" + dogname);

}

public void initAge(int dogage){

    dogAge = dogage;

}

public int getDogAge( ){

```java
        System.out.println("Dog's present age is:" + dogAge );

        return dogAge;

}

public static void main(String []args){

        Dog myDog = new Dog( "jimmy" );

        myDog.initAge( 5 );

        myDog.getDogAge( );

        System.out.println("Variable    dogAge    Value    is:"    + myDog.dogAge );

}

}
```

Upon compilation and execution of the following code, you shall be able to see the following result.

Variable dogAge Value is: 5

Declaration Guidelines for Source Files

As the last piece of this area how about we now investigate the source file declaration standards. These tenets are key when declaring classes, importing declarations and packages in a source file.

- There can be stand out public class for every source record.
- A source document can have numerous non public classes.

- The public class name ought to be the name of the source document. The name of the source file must be affixed by the string .java. For instance, the class name is public class Employeerecord{}, then the source document ought to be saved as Employeerecord.java.
- If the class is declared inside a package, then the package articulation ought to be the first proclamation in the source record.
- If import articulations are available, then they must be composed between the package proclamation and the class revelation. On the off chance that there are no package proclamations, then the import articulation ought to be the first line in the source file.
- Import and package articulations will intimate to all the classes show in the source record. It is impractical to announce diverse import and/or package explanations to distinctive classes in the source file.

Classes have a few access levels. Moreover, there are diverse sorts of classes, which include final classes, in addition to several others. Separated from the aforementioned sorts of classes, Java likewise has some uncommon classes called Inner classes and Anonymous classes.

Java Packages

Basically, it is a method for classifying the classes and interfaces. At the point when creating applications in Java, many classes and interfaces will be composed. In such a scenario, ordering these classes is an unquestionable requirement and makes life much less demanding. In Java, if a completely qualified name, which incorporates the class and package name, is given, then the compiler can without much of a stretch find the source code or classes. Import declarations is a method for giving the correct area for the compiler to find that specific class.

Case in point, in order to load all the classes accessible in java_installation/java/io, you must use the following statement:

import java.io.*;

A sample implementation for this concept is given below:

The following code uses two classes Employeerecord and Employeerecordtest. The first step is to open the text editor you intend to use at your system and copy and paste the code shown below into the text editor application. Keep in mind that the public class in the code is Employeerecord. Therefore, the name of the file should be Employeerecord.java. This class uses the variables, methods and constructor as shown below:

import java.io.*;

public class Employeerecord {

int empage;

String empname;

double empcompensation;

```
public Employee(string empname){

this.empname = empname;

}

public void employeeage(int employeeage){

empage = employeeage;

}

public void empcompensation(double empcompensation){

empcompensation = empcompensation;

}

public void printemp(){

System.out.println("empname:"+ empname );

System.out.println("empage:" + empage );

System.out.println("empcompensation:" + empcompensation);

}
```

As specified awhile ago in this exercise, handling begins from the main function. Accordingly, with this goal, we should create a main function for this Employeerecord class. Given beneath is the Employeerecordtest class, which makes two instances of the class Employeerecord and conjures the techniques for each one item to allot values for every variable. You can save this file as Employeerecordtest.java.

```java
import java.io.*;

public class Employeerecordtest{

public static void main(String args[]){

Employeerecord employee1 = new Employeerecord("Jack Wright");

Employeerecord employee2 = new Employeerecord("Mary John");

employee1.employeeage(32);

employee1.empcompensation(5000);

employee2.employeeage(25);

employee2.empcompensation(2000);

employee1.printemp();

employee2.printemp();

}

}
```

Upon compilation and execution, you must get the following output:

empname: Jack Wright

empage: 32

empcompensation: 5000

empname: Mary John

empage: 25

empcompensation: 2000

Basic Data Types

Variables are only saved memory areas to store values. This implies that when you make a variable, you save some space in memory. In light of the data type of a variable, the working framework distributes memory and chooses what can be put in the held memory. Consequently, by appointing diverse data types to variables, you can store whole numbers, decimals, or characters in these variables.

There are two data types accessible in Java:

- Reference/Object Data Types
- Primitive Data Types

Primitive Data Types

There are eight primitive information types, which are supported by Java. Primitive data types are predefined by the dialect and named by a catchphrase. This section discusses these data types in detail.

byte:

- byte information sort is a 8-bit marked two's supplement whole number.
- Maximum worth is $2^7 -1$, which is equal to 127. This value is also included in the range of these values.
- Minimum worth is -2^7, which is equal to -128.
- Default value stored in a variable of this type is 0.

- byte information sort is utilized to spare space in vast exhibits, principally set up of numbers, since a byte is four times littler than an int.
- Example:
  byte x = 200, byte y = -20

short:

- short information sort is a 16-bit marked two's supplement number.
- Maximum value is 2^15 -1, which is equal to 32,767. This number is also included in the range.
- Minimum value is -2^15, which is equal to -32,768.
- short information sort can likewise be utilized to spare memory as byte information sort. A short is 2 times littler than an int
- The default value for this data type is 0.
- Example:
  short x = 425164, short y = -76686

int:

- int information sort is a 32-bit marked two's supplement number.
- Maximum value for this data type is 2^31 -1, which is equal to 2,147,483,647. This number is also included in the range for this data type.
- Minimum value for this data type is -2^31, which is equal to -2,147,483,648.

- int is for the most part utilized as the default information sort for its indispensable qualities unless there is a worry about memory.
- The default value for this data type is 0.
- Example:
  int x = 826378, int y = -64782

long:

- long information sort is a 64-bit marked two's supplement whole number.
- Maximum value for this data type is $2^{63} -1$, which is equal to 9,223,372,036,854,775,807.
- Minimum value for this data type is -2^{63}, which is equal to -9,223,372,036,854,775,808.
- This sort is utilized when a more extensive memory range than int is required.
- The default value for those data type is 0l.
- Example:
  long x = 174636l, int y = -536452l

float:

- float is a data type, which is know for its solitary exactness, 32-bit IEEE 754 gliding point.
- float is for the most part used to spare memory in vast exhibits of coasting point numbers.
- The default value for this data type is 0.0f.

- float information sort is never utilized for exact values, for example, money.
- Example:
float x = 254.3f

double:

- double information sort is a float with twofold exactness 64-bit IEEE 754 drifting point.
- This information sort is for the most part utilized as the default information sort for decimal qualities.
- double information sort ought to never be utilized for exact values, for example, money.
- The default value for this data type is 0.0d.
- Example:
double x = 321.4

boolean:

- boolean information sort speaks to one bit of data.
- Any boolean variable can assume one of the two values: true or false.
- This information sort is utilized for basic banners that track genuine/false conditions.
- The default value for this data type is false.
- Example:
boolean check = true;

char:

- char information sort is a solitary 16-bit Unicode character.
- Maximum value for a variable of this type is "\uffff" (or 65,535 comprehensive).
- Minimum value for a variable of this type is "\u0000" (or 0).
- char information sort is utilized to store any character.
- example:
  char text ='a'

Reference Data Types

- Reference variables are made utilizing characterized constructors of the classes. They are utilized to get to objects. These variables are proclaimed to be of a particular data type that can't be changed. A few examples of such data types are Employee and Dog.
- Class objects, and different kind of variables go under reference data type.
- Default estimation of any reference variable is invalid.
- A reference variable can be utilized to allude to any object of the announced sort.
- Example: myanimal = new Animals("rabbit");

Java Literals

A literal in Java is a source code representation of a settled worth. They are spoken to specifically in the code without any calculation. Literals can be appointed to any primitive sort variable. Case in point:

byte x = 86;

char x = "a"

int, byte, short and long can be communicated in hexadecimal(base 16), decimal(base 10) or octal(base 8) number frameworks too. Prefix 0 is utilized to show octal while prefix 0x demonstrates hexadecimal when utilizing these number frameworks for literals. For example,

int numd = 134;

int numo = 0243;

int numx = 0x95;

String literals in Java are determined like they are in most different programming languages by encasing a grouping of characters between a couple of twofold quotes. Illustrations of string literals are:

"Hi Everyone" "two\nlines" "\"these characters are inside quotes\""

String sorts of literals can contain any Unicode characters. For instance:

String news = "\u0001"

You can also use escape sequences with Java. Here is a list of escape sequences that you can use.

Double quote - \"
Carriage return (0x0d) - \r
Newline (0x0a) - \n
Single quote - \'
Backspace (0x08) - \b

Formfeed (0x0c) - \f

Tab - \t

Space (0x20) - \s

Octal character (ddd) - \ddd

Backslash - \\

Hexadecimal UNICODE character (xxxx) - \uxxxx

Variable Types

A variable gives us named capacity that our code can control. Every variable in Java has a particular sort, which decides the size and format of the variable's memory; the scope of values that can be put away inside that memory; and the set of operations that can be connected to the variable. You must make an explicit declaration of all variables before they can be utilized. Variables can be declared in the following manner:

Data type <variable name>;

Here data type is one of Java's datatypes. On the other hand, a variable is the name or the identifier associated with the variable. To pronounce more than one variable of the pointed out type, you can utilize a comma-divided rundown. Here are a few examples of declarations:

The following declaration declares three integer variables.

int x, y, z;

In a similar manner, variables of other data types may also be declared.

Java supports three types of variables. These types are as follows:

- Class/static variables
- Instance variables
- Local variables

Local Variables

- Local variables are announced in systems, constructors, or scopes.
- Local variables are made when the constructor or method is entered and the variable will be decimated once it retreats the system, constructor or scope.
- Access modifiers can't be utilized for neighborhood variables.
- Local variables are noticeable just inside the announced method, constructor or scope.
- Local variables are executed at stack level.
- There is no default value for these variables. So, local variables ought to be declared and a beginning value ought to be relegated before the first utilization.

Sample Implementation:

Here, age is a neighborhood variable. This is characterized inside pupage() strategy and its degree is constrained to this system just.

public class myTest{

open void newfunc(){

int myvar = 1;

myvar = myvar + 10;

System.out.println("The value of myvar is: " + myvar);

}

```
public static void main(string args[]){

mytest = new myTest ();

mytest.myfunc();

}
```

The output of the execution of this code is:

The value of myvar is: 11

Instance Variables

- The declaration of an instance variable is made inside the class. However, it is made outside the system, constructor or any scope.
- Instance variables are made when an object is made with the utilization of the keyword "new" and obliterated when the item is destroyed.
- When a space is dispensed for an item in the memory, an opening for each one variable value is made.
- Instance variables can be pronounced in class level before or after utilization.
- Instance variables hold values that must be referenced by more than one method, constructor or piece, or key parts of an object's express that must be available all through the class.
- Access modifiers can be given for sample variables.
- Instance variables have default values. For numbers, the default quality is 0. However, for Booleans, it is false and for object

references, it is invalid. Qualities can be relegated amid the statement or inside the constructor.

- The case variables are unmistakable for all methods, constructors and scope in the class. Regularly, it is prescribed to make these variables private (access level). However perceivability for subclasses can be given with the utilization of access modifiers for these variables.
- Instance variables can be gotten to by calling the variable name inside the class. The following statement can be used for this purpose: Objectreference.variablename.

Sample Implementation:

import java.io.*;

public class Employeerecord{

public String empname;

private double empcompensation;

public Employee (String name){

empname = name;

}

public void initsalary(double empsalary){

empcompensation = empsalary;

}

```java
public void printemployee(){

System.out.println("Employee name  : " + empname );

System.out.println("Employee salary :" + empcompensation);

}

public static void main(string args[]){

Employeerecord employee1 = new Employeerecord("Mary");

employee1.initsalary(7500);

employee1.printemployee();

}
```

The compilation and execution would deliver the accompanying result:

Employee name : Mary

Employee compensation :7500.0

Class/Static Variables

- Class variables otherwise called static variables are declared with the static keyword in a class, yet outside a constructor, method or scope.
- There would just be one duplicate of each class variable for every class, paying little mind to what number of objects are made from it.

- Static variables are seldom utilized other than being pronounced as constants. Constants are variables that are announced as private/public, static and final. Consistent variables never show signs of change from their introductory quality.
- Static variables are put away in static memory. It is uncommon to utilize static variables other than announced final and utilized as either private or public constants.
- Static variables are made when the system begins and annihilated when the execution stops.
- Visibility is like instance variables. In any case, most static variables are announced public since they must be accessible for clients of the class.
- Default values for these variables are also same as instance variables. For numbers, the default value id typically 0. However, the same value for Booleans is false and for object reference is invalid. Values can be doled out amid the assertion or inside the constructor. Furthermore, values can be appointed in unique static initializer brackets.
- Static variables can be gotten to by calling with the class name . Classname.variablename.
- When announcing class variables as public static final, variables names (constants) must all be in upper case. Moreover, the static variables are not public and the naming convention is the same as local and instance variables.

Sample Implementation:

```java
import java.io.*;

public class Employeerecord{

private static double empcompensation;

public static final String empdept = "HR ";

public static void main(string args[]){

empcomp = 7500;

System.out.println(empdept+" Compensation: "+empcompensation);

}
```

The compilation and execution of this code shall create the accompanying result:

HR Compensation: 7500

Modifier Types

Modifiers are catchphrases that you add to definitions to change their implications. The Java programming language has a wide and mixed bag of modifiers, including the accompanying:

- Non-Access Modifiers
- Java Access Modifiers

In order to utilize a modifier, you incorporate its catchphrase in the meaning of a class, variable or method. The modifier goes before whatever is left of the announcement.

Access Control Modifiers:

Java gives various access modifiers to set access levels for classes, variables, routines and constructors. The four right to gain access are:

- Private: visible to the class.
- Default: visible to the bundle. No modifiers are required.
- Secured: visible to all subclasses and package.
- Public: visible to the world.

Non Access Modifiers:

Java gives various non-access modifiers to attain numerous other usefulness.

- Static:
  The static modifier for making class variables and methods.
- Final
  The final modifier for concluding the executions of classes, variables and methods.
- Abstract
  This modifier is used for for creating abstract methods and classes.
- Volatile and Synchronized
  These modifiers are typically used for threads.

Operators in Java

The operator set in Java is extremely rich. Broadly, the operators available in Java are divided in the following categories.

- Relational Operators
- Arithmetic Operators
- Logical Operators
- Bitwise Operators
- Misc Operators
- Assignment Operators

The Arithmetic Operators

Operations in Java are used in essentially the same manner as in algebra. They are used with variables for performing arithmetic operations. Here is a list of arithmetic operators available in Java.

Operation	Operator	Description
Addition	+	Adds the values of two variables
Subtraction	-	Subtracts the values of two variables
Multiplication	*	Multiplies the values of two variables
Division	/	Divides the values of two variables
Modulus	%	The resultant value is the remainder of division
Increment	++	Increases the value by 1
Decrement	--	Decreases the value by 1

The Relational Operators

Java also supports several relational operators. The list of relational operators that are supported by Java are given below.

Operation	Operator	Description
Equal To	==	Compares the values of two variables for equality
Not Equal To	!=	Compares the values of two variables for inequality
Greater Than	>	Checks if one value is greater than the other value
Lesser Than	<	Checks if one value is lesser than the other value
Greater Than Or Equal To	>=	Checks if one value is greater than or equal to the other value
Lesser Than Or Equal To	<=	Checks if one value is lesser than or equal to the other value

The Bitwise Operators

The bitwise operators available in Java can be easily applied to a number of data types. These data types include byte, short, long, int and char. Typically, any bitwise operator performs the concerned operation bit-wise. For instance, if you consider the example of an integer x, which has the value 60. Therefore, the binary equivalent of x is 00111100. Consider another variable y, with the value 13 or 00001101. If we perform the bitwise operation & on these two numbers, then you will get the following result:

x&y = 0000 1100

The table shown below shows a list of bitwise operators that are available in Java.

Operation	Operator	Description
BINARY AND	&	Performs the AND operation
BINARY OR	|	Performs the OR operation
BINARY XOR	^	Performs the XOR operation
ONE'S COMPLEMENT	~	Performs the complementation operation on a unary variable
BINARY LEFT SHIFT	<<	Performs the left shifting of bits
BINARY RIGHT SHIFT	>>	Performs the right shifting of bits

In addition to the above mentioned, Java also supports right shift zero fill operator (>>>), which fills the shifted bits on the right with zero.

The Logical Operators

Logical operators are an integral part of any operator set. The logical operators supported by Java are listed in the table below.

Operation	Operator	Description
Logical AND	&&	Returns True if both the

		conditions mentioned are true
Logical OR	||	Returns True if one or both the conditions mentioned are true
Logical NOT	!	Returns True if the condition mentioned is False

The Assignment Operators

There are following assignment operators supported by Java language:

Operation	Operator	Description
Simple assignment operator	=	Assigns a value on the right to the variable in the left
Add - assignment operator	+=	Adds the value on the right to the value of the variable on the left and assigns the resultant to the variable on the left
Subtract assignment operator	-=	Subtracts the value on the right to the value of the variable on the left and assigns the resultant to the variable on the left
Multiply assignment operator	*=	Multiplies the value on the right to the value of the variable on the left and assigns the resultant

		to the variable on the left
Divide - assignment operator	/=	Divides the value on the right to the value of the variable on the left and assigns the resultant to the variable on the left
Modulus - assignment operator	%=	It takes the modulus of the LHS and RHS and assigns the resultant to the variable on the left
Left shift - assignment operator	<<=	It takes the left shift of the LHS and RHS and assigns the resultant to the variable on the left
Right shift - assignment operator	>>=	It takes the right shift of the LHS and RHS and assigns the resultant to the variable on the left
Bitwise - assignment operator	&=	It takes the bitwise AND of the LHS and RHS and assigns the resultant to the variable on the left
bitwise exclusive OR - assignment operator	^=	It takes the bitwise XOR of the LHS and RHS and assigns the resultant to the variable on the

		left	
bitwise inclusive OR - assignment operator	|=	It takes the bitwise OR of the LHS and RHS and assigns the resultant to the variable on the left	

Misc Operators

In addition to the above mentioned, there are several other operators, which are supported by Java.

Conditional Operator (? :):

The conditional operator is a ternary operator that contains three operands. Essentially, this operator is used for the evaluation of boolean expressions. The operator tests the first operand or condition and if the condition is true, then the second value is assigned to the variable. However, if the condition is false, the third operand is assigned to the variable. The syntax of this operator is as follows:

variable a = (<condition>) ? valueiftrue : valueiffalse

Sample implementation:

public class myTest {

public static void main(String args[]){

int x, y;

x = 5;

```
y = (x == 5) ? 15: 40;

System.out.println( "y = " + y );

y = (x == 34) ? 60: 95;

System.out.println( "x = " + y );

    }

}
```

The compilation and execution of this code shall give the following result:

y = 15

y = 95

instanceof Operator:

Only object reference variables can be used with this operator. The objective of this operator is to check is an object is an instance of an exiting class. The syntax of this operator is as follows:

(<object reference variable>) instanceof(<interface/class>)

Sample implementation of this operator and its purpose of use is given below:

```
public class myTest {

public static void main(String args[]){

int x = 4;
```

```java
boolean resultant = x instanceof int;

System.out.println( resultant );

}

}
```

The output of this code shall be true. This operator can also be used in comparison. A sample implementation of this is given below:

```java
class Animal {}

public class Monkey extends Animal {

public static void main(String args[]){

Animal newa = new Monkey();

boolean resultant = newa instanceof Monkey;

System.out.println( resultant );

}

}
```

The output for this code will also be true.

Precedence of Java Operators

More often than not, operators are used in combinations in expressions. However, you must have also realized that it becomes difficult to predict the order in which operations will take place during execution. The operator precedence table for Java shall help you predict operator operations in an expression deduction. For instance, if you are performing addition and multiplication in the same expression, then multiplication takes place prior to addition. The following table illustrates the order and hierarchy of operators in Java. The associativity for all the operators is left to right. However, the unary, assignment and conditional operator follows right to left associativity.

Operator	Category
() [] . (dot operator)	Postfix
++ -- ! ~	Unary
* / %	Multiplicative
+ -	Additive
>> >>> <<	Shift
> >= < <=	Relational
== !=	Equality
&	Bitwise AND
|	Bitwise OR
^	Bitwise XOR
&&	Logical AND
||	Logical OR
?:	Conditional

= += -= *= /= %= >>= <<= &= ^= |=	Assignment
,	Comma

Loops in Java

Looping is a common programming situation that you can expect to encounter rather regularly. Loop can simply be described as a situation in which you may need to execute the same block of code over and over. Java supports three looping constructs, which are as follows:

- for Loop
- do...while Loop
- while Loop

In addition to this, the foreach looping construct also exists. However, this construct will be explained in the chapter on arrays.

The while Loop:

A while loop is a control structure that permits you to rehash an errand a specific number of times. The syntax for this construct is as follows:

while(boolean_expression) {

/Statements

}

At the point when executing, if the boolean_expression result is genuine, then the activities inside the circle will be executed. This will proceed till the time the result for the condition is genuine. Here, key purpose of the while loop is that the circle may not ever run. At the point when the interpretation is tried and the result is false, the body of the loop will be skipped and the first proclamation after the while circle will be executed.

Sample:

public class myTest {

public static void main(string args[]) {

int i=5;

while(i<10) {

System.out.print(" i = " + i);

i++;

System.out.print("\n");

}

}

This would deliver the accompanying result:

x = 5

x = 6

x = 7

x = 8

x = 9

x = 5

The do...while Loop

A do...while loop is similar to the while looping construct aside from that a do...while circle is ensured to execute no less than one time. The syntax for this looping construct is as follows:

do {

/Statements

}while(<booleanexpression>);

Perceive that the Boolean declaration shows up toward the end of the circle, so the code execute once before the Boolean is tried. In the event that the Boolean declaration is genuine, the stream of control bounced go down to do, and the code execute once more. This methodology rehashes until the Boolean articulation is false.

Sample implementation:

public class myTest {

public static void main(string args[]){

int i = 1;

do{

System.out.print("i = " + i);

i++; System.out.print("\n");

}while(i<1);

}

This would create the accompanying result:

i = 1

The for Loop

A for circle is a reiteration control structure that permits you to effectively compose a loop that needs to execute a particular number of times. A for looping construct is helpful when you know how often an errand is to be rehashed. The syntax for the looping construct is as follows:

The punctuation of a for circle is:

for(initialization; Boolean_expression; redesign)

{

/Statements

}

Here is the stream of control in a for circle:

- The introduction step is executed in the first place, and just once. This step permits you to pronounce and introduce any loop control variables. You are not needed to put an announcement here, the length of a semicolon shows up.

- Next, the Boolean outflow is assessed. In the event that it is genuine, the assemblage of the loop is executed. In the event that it is false, the assortment of the loop does not execute and stream of control hops to the following articulation past the for circle.
- After the group of the for circle executes, the stream of control bounced down to the overhaul explanation. This announcement permits you to overhaul any circle control variables. This announcement can be left clear, the length of a semicolon shows up after the Boolean declaration.
- The Boolean outflow is currently assessed once more. On the off chance that it is genuine, the loop executes and the scope rehashes itself. After the Boolean declaration is false, the for loop ends.

Sample Implementation

```
public class myTest {

public static void main(string args[]) {

for(int i = 0; i < 5; i = i+1) {

System.out.print("i = " + i );

System.out.print("\n");

}

}
```

This would deliver the accompanying result:

i = 0

i = 1

i = 2

i = 3

i = 4

Extended Version of for Loop in Java

As of Java 5, the upgraded for loop was presented. This is basically utilized for Arrays. The syntax for this loop is as follows:

for(declaration : statement)

{

//Statements

}

- Declaration: The recently declared variable, which is of a sort perfect with the components of the show you are getting to. The variable will be accessible inside the for piece and its esteem would be the same as the current array component.
- Expression: This assesses to the exhibit you have to loop through. The interpretation can be an array variable or function call that returns an array.

Sample Implementation:

```
public class myTest {

public static void main(string args[]){

int [] mynumber = {0, 5, 10, 15, 20};

for(int i : mynumber ){

System.out.print( i );

System.out.print(" ,");

}

}
```

This would deliver the accompanying result:

0, 5, 10, 15, 20

The break Keyword

The break keyword is utilized to stop the whole loop execution. The break word must be utilized inside any loop or a switch construct. The break keyword will stop the execution of the deepest circle and begin executing the following line of code after the ending curly bracket. The syntax for using this keyword is as follows:

break;

Sample Implementation:

```java
public class myTest {

public static void main(string args[]) {

int [] mynumbers = {0, 5, 10, 15, 20};

for(int i : mynumbers ) {

if( i == 15 ) {

break;

}

System.out.print( i );

System.out.print("\n");

}

}
```

This would deliver the accompanying result:

0

5

10

The Continue Keyword

The proceed with decisive word can be utilized as a part of any of the loop control structures. It causes the loop to quickly bounce to the following emphasis of the loop.

- In a for circle, the continue keyword reasons stream of control to quickly bounce to the overhaul articulation.
- In a while or do/while loop, stream of control instantly hops to the Boolean interpretation.

The syntax of using this keyword is as follows:

continue;

Sample Implementation:

public class myTest {

public static void main(String args[]) {

int [] mynumbers = {0, 5, 10, 15, 20};

for(int i : mynumbers) {

if(i == 15) {

continue;

}

System.out.print(i);

System.out.print("\n");

}

}

}

The expected output of the code is:

0

5

10

20

Decision Making

There are two sorts of decision making constructs in Java. They are:

- if constructs
- switch constructs

The if Statement:

An if constructs comprises of a Boolean outflow emulated by one or more proclamations. The syntax for using this construct is as follows:

if(<condition>) {

//Statements if the condition is true

}

In the event that the Boolean construct assesses to true, then the scope of code inside the if proclamation will be executed. If not the first set of code after the end of the if construct (after the end wavy prop) will be executed.

Sample Implementation:

public class myTest {

public static void main(string args[]){

int i = 0;

if(i < 1){

System.out.print("The if construct is executing!");

}

}

This would create the accompanying result:

The if construct is executing!

The if...else Statement

An if proclamation can be trailed by a non-compulsory else explanation, which executes when the Boolean outflow is false. The syntax for this construct is as follows:

if(<condition>){

//Executes if condition is true

}

else{

//Executes if condition is false

}

Sample Implementation:

public class myTest {

public static void main(string args[]){

int i = 0;

if(i > 1){

System.out.print("The if construct is executing!");

}

else{

System.out.print("The else construct is executing!");

}

}

This would create the accompanying result:

The else construct is executing!

The if...else if Statement

An if proclamation can be trailed by a non-compulsory else if...else explanation, which is exceptionally helpful to test different conditions utilizing single if...else if articulation.

At the point when utilizing if , else if , else proclamations there are few focuses to remember.

- An if can have zero or one else's and it must come after any else if's.
- An if can have zero to numerous else if's and they must precede the else.
- If one of the if conditions yield a true, the other else ifs and else are ignored.

The syntax for using this decision making construct Is as follows:

```
if(condition_1){

//Execute if condition_1 is true

}

else if(condition_2){

//Execute if condition_2 is true

}

else if(condition_3){

//Execute if condition_3 is true

}

else

{

//Execute if all conditions are false

}
```

Sample Implementation:

```
public class myTest {

public static void main(string args[]){

int i = 0;

if( i > 1 ){
```

```
System.out.print("The first if construct is executing!");

}

else if(i == 0){

System.out.print("The second if construct is executing!");

}

else{

System.out.print("The else construct is executing!");

}

}
```

This would create the accompanying result:

The second if construct is executing!

Nested if...else Statement

It is legitimate to home if-else constructs, which implies you can utilize one if or else if proclamation inside an alternate if or else if explanation. The syntax for using this construct Is as follows:

```
if(condition_1){

//Execute if condition_1 is true

    if(condition_2){

    //Execute if condition_2 is true
```

```
    }
}
else if(condition_3){
//Execute if condition_3 is true
}
else
{
//Execute if all conditions are false
}
```

Sample Implementation:

```
public class myTest {
public static void main(string args[]){
int i = 1;
if( i >= 1 ){
System.out.println("The if construct is executing!");
    if(i == 1){
    System.out.println("The nested if construct is executing!");
    }
```

}

else{

System.out.print("The else construct is executing!");

}

}

This would create the accompanying result:

The if construct is executing!

The nested if construct is executing!

The switch Statement

A switch construct permits a variable to be tried for equity against a rundown of values. Each one value is known as a case, and the variable being exchanged on is checked for each one case. The syntax for using this decision making construct is as follows:

switch(<condition>){

case value1:

//Statements

break;

case value2 :

//Statements

```
break;

default:

//Optional

}
```

The accompanying runs apply to a switch construct:

- The variable utilized as a part of a switch explanation must be a short, byte, char or int.
- You can have any number of case explanations inside a switch. Each one case is trailed by the value to be contrasted with and a colon.
- The value for a case must be the same type as the variable in the switch and it must be a steady or an exacting value.
- When the variable being exchanged on is equivalent to a case, the announcements after that case will execute until a break is arrived at.
- When a break is arrived at, the switch ends, and the stream of control bounces to the following line after the switch.
- Not each case needs to contain a break. In the event that no break shows up, the stream of control will fall through to consequent cases until a break is arrived at.
- A switch articulation can have a discretionary default case, which must show up toward the end of the switch. The default case can be utilized for performing an undertaking when none of the cases is true. No break is required in the default case.

However, as per the convention, the use of the same is recommended.

Sample Implementation:

```java
public class myTest {

public static void main(string args[]){

char mygrade = 'A';

switch(mygrade)

{

case "A" :

System.out.println("Excellent Performance!");

break;

case "B" :

System.out.println("Good Performance!");

break;

default :

System.out.println("Failed");

}
```

Aggregate and run above code utilizing different inputs to grade. This would create the accompanying result for the present value of mygrade:

Excellent Performance!

Strings in Java

Strings, which are generally utilized as a part of Java, for writing computer programs, are a grouping of characters. In the Java programming language, strings are like everything else, objects. The Java platform provides the String class to make and control strings.

Instantiating Strings

The most appropriate approach to make a string is to use the following statement:

String mystring = "Hi world!";

At whatever point it experiences a string exacting in your code, the compiler makes a String object with its value for this situation, "Hi world!'.

Similarly as with other objects, you can make Strings by utilizing a constructor and a new keyword. The String class has eleven constructors that permit you to give the starting estimation of the string utilizing diverse sources, for example, a cluster of characters.

public class myStringdemo{

public static void main(string args[]){

char[] myarray = { 'h', 'i', '.'};

String mystring = new String(myarray);

System.out.println(mystring);

}

This would deliver the accompanying result:

hi.

Note: The String class is changeless, so that once it is made a String object, its type can't be changed. In the event that there is a need to make a great deal of alterations to Strings of characters, then you ought to utilize String Buffer & String Builder Classes.

Determining String Length

Routines used to get data about an object are known as accessor methods. One accessor technique that you can use with strings is the length() function, which furnishes a proportional payback of characters contained in the string item. This function can be utilized in the following manner:

public class mystring {

public static void main(string args[]) {

String newstr = "I am hungry!";

int strlen = newstr.length();

System.out.println("length = " + strlen); }

This would create the accompanying result:

length = 12

How to Concatenate Strings

The String class incorporates a function for connecting two strings:

mystring1.concat(mystring2);

This returns another string that is mystring1 with mystring2 added to it toward the end. You can likewise utilize the concat() system with string literals, as in:

"My name is ".concat("mary");

Strings are all the more usually concatenated with the + administrator, as in:

"Hi," + " world" + "!"

which brings about:

"Hi, world!"

Sample Implementation:

public class MyString {

public static void main(string args[]) {

String mystr = "Sorry";

System.out.println("I " + "am " + mystr);

}

This would deliver the accompanying result:

I am Sorry

Format Strings

You have format() and printf() functions to print the output with designed numbers. The function format() of the String class returns a String object as against a Printstream object. This function creates a formatted string that can be reused. This function can be used in the following manner:

String fstr;

fstr = String.format("Float variable value " + "%f, and Integer value " + "variable is %d, and the contents of the string is " + " %s", fVar, iVar, sVar);

System.out.println(fstr);

String Methods

This section contains a list of methods that are available as part of the String class.

int compareTo(Object obj) – This function compares the specified string with the object concerned.

char charAt(int chindex) – This function returns the char present at the index value 'index.'

int compareToIgnoreCase(String mystr) – This function performs the lexographic comparison of the two strings. However, the case differences are ignored by this function.

int compareTo(String aString) – This function performs the lexographic comparison between the strings.

boolean contentEquals(StringBuffer strb) – This function checks if the string is same as the sequence of characters present in the StringBuffer. It returns true on success and false on failure.

String concat(String strnext) – This function appends the string with another string at the end.

static String copyValueOf(char[] mydata, int xoffset, int xcount) – This function returns a stringf, which is indicative of the character sequence in the original string.

static String copyValueOf(char[] newdata) – This function copies the string of characters into a character buffer in the form of a sequence of characters.

boolean equals(Object aObject) – This function compares the object with the string concerned.

boolean endsWith(String newsuffix) – This function appends the string with the specified suffix.

byte getBytes() – Using this function, the string can be encoded into bytes format, which are stored in a resultant array.

boolean equalsIgnoreCase(String aString) – This function makes a comparison of the two strings without taking the case of characters into consideration.

void getChars(int srcBegin, int sourceEnd, char[] dst, int destinationBegin) – This function copies characters from the specified beginning character to the end character into an array.

byte[] getBytes(String charsetnm) - Using this function, the string can be encoded into bytes format using named char set, which are stored in a resultant array.

int indexOf(int charx) – This function returns the index of first character that is same as the character specified in the function call.

int hashCode() – A hash code is returned by this string.

int indexOf(String newstr) - This function returns the index of the first occurrence of a substring in a string.

int indexOf(int charx, int fromIndexloc) – This function returns the index of first character that is same as the character specified in the function call. The search starts from the specified index.

String intern() – A canonical representation of a string object given in the function call is returned.

int indexOf(String newstr, int fromIndexloc) - This function returns the index of the first occurrence of a substring in a string. The search starts from the specified index.

int lastIndexOf(int charx, int fromIndexloc) - This function makes a search for a character from the specified index and returns the index where the last occurrence is found.

int lastIndexOf(int charx) - This function makes a search for a character backwards and returns the index where the last occurrence or first occurrence in a backward search is found.

int lastIndexOf(String newstr, int fromIndexloc) – This function makes a search for a sub-string from the specified index and returns the index where the last occurrence is found.

int lastIndexOf(String newstr) - This function makes a search for a sub-string backwards and returns the index where the last occurrence or first occurrence in a backward search is found.

boolean matches(String aregex) - – This function checks for equality between a string region and a regular expression.

int length() – This function calculates and returns the string length.

boolean regionMatches(int totaloffset, String otherstr, int otheroffset, int strlen) – This function checks for equality between string regions.

boolean regionMatches(boolean ignorecharcase, int totaloffset, String otherstr, int otheroffset, int strlen) – This function checks for equality between string regions.

String replace(char oldCharx, char newCharx) - This function looks for a substring that matches the regular expression and then replaces all the occurrences with the specified string. The function returns the resultant string, which is obtained after making all the replacements.

String replaceFirst(String newregex, String newreplacement) – This function looks for a substring that matches the regular expression and then replaces the first occurrence with the specified string.

String replaceAll(String newregex, String xreplacement) - This function looks for a substring that matches the regular expression and then replaces all the occurrences with the specified string.

String[] split(String newregex, int xlimit) – This function performs splitting of the string according to the regular expression with it and the given limit.

String[] split(String newregex) - This function performs splitting of the string according to the regular expression with it.

boolean startsWith(String newprefix, int totaloffset) – This function checks if the given string has the prefix at the specified index.

boolean startsWith(String newprefix) – This function checks if the given string begins with the prefix sent with the function call.

String substring(int beginIndexloc) - This function returns a string, which is substring of the specified string. The substring is determined by the beginning index to the end of the string.

CharSequence subSequence(int beginIndexloc, int endIndexloc) - This function returns a character sequence, which is sub-character sequence of the specified character sequence. The substring is determined by the beginning and ending indexes.

char[] toCharArray() – This function performs the conversion of a string to a character array.

String substring(int beginIndexloc, int endIndexloc) – This function returns a string, which is substring of the specified string. The substring is determined by the beginning and ending index.

String toLowerCase(Locale localenew) - This function converts all the characters in the specified string to lower case using given locale rules.

String toLowerCase() - This function converts all the characters in the specified string to lower case using default locale rules.

String toUpperCase() - This function converts all the characters in the specified string to upper case using default locale rules.

String toString() – This function returns the string itself.

String toUpperCase(Locale localenew) – This function converts all the characters in the specified string to upper case using locale rules.

static String valueOf(primitive data type x) – A string representation is returned by this function.

String trim() – Omits the whitespace that trails and leads a string.

Arrays

Java supports an information structure, which is similar to a cluster. This information structure is called an array. It is capable of storing an altered size successive accumulation of components of the same data type. An array is utilized to store an accumulation of information, yet it is frequently more valuable to think about it as an exhibit for storing variables of the same sort.

As opposed to making declarations of individual variables, for example, num0, num1 and num99, you can declare one array variable. For example, an array of four elements is declared as arrayname[4]. This chapter discusses all the facets of array declaration, access and manipulation.

How To Declare array Variables

To utilize an array as a part of a system, you must declare a variable to reference the array. Besides this, you must determine the sort of array the variable can reference. Here is the syntax for declaring a variable of the type array:

datatype[] myarray;

Sample Implementation:

The accompanying code bits are illustrations of this concept:

double[] myarray;

Making Arrays

You can make an exhibit by utilizing the new operator with the accompanying statement:

myarray = new datatype[sizeofarray];

The above declaration does two things:

- It makes an exhibit with the help of the new operator in the following manner:

  new datatype[arraysize];

- It relegates the reference of the recently made array to the variable myarray.

Proclaiming a array variable, making an exhibit, and doling out the reference of the show to the variable can be consolidated in one declaration, as appeared:

datatype[] myarray = new datatype[sizeofarray];

On the other hand, you can also make clusters in the following manner:

datatype[] myarray = {val0, val1, ..., valk};

The components of the array are gotten to through the record. Array lists are 0-based; that is, they begin from 0 to go up to myarray.length-1.

Sample Implementation:

The declaration shown below declares an array, myarray, makes a cluster of 10 components of double type and doles out its reference to myarray:

double[] myarray = new double[10];

Handling Arrays

At the point when handling components of an array, we frequently utilize either for or foreach in light of the fact that the majority of the components in an array are of the same sort and the extent of the exhibit is known.

Example:

public class Mytestarray {

```
public static void main(string[] args) {
double[] myarray = {0.5, 1.2, 2.2, 3.4, 4.7};
for (int k = 0; k < myarray.length; k++) {
System.out.println(myarray[k] + " ");
}
double aggregate = 0;
for (int k = 0; k < myarray.length; k++) {
aggregate += myarray[k];
}
System.out.println("Aggregate value = " + aggregate);
double maxval = myarray[0];
for (int k = 1; k < mylist.length; k++) {
if (myarray[i] > maxval)
maxval = myarray[k];
}
System.out.println("Max Value is " + maxval);
}
```

This would create the accompanying result:

0.5 1.2 2.2 3.4 4.7

Aggregate = 12.0

Max Value is 4.7

The foreach Loops

JDK 1.5 presented another for construct, which is known as foreach loop or extended for loop. This construct empowers you to cross the complete array successively without utilizing an extra variable.

Sample Implementation:

```
public class Mytestarray {
```

```
public static void main(string[] args) {
double[] myarray = {0.5, 1.2, 2.2, 3.4, 4.7};
for (double i: myarray) {
System.out.println(i);
}
}
```

This would deliver the accompanying result:

0.5 1.2 2.2 3.4 4.7

Passing Arrays to Methods:

Generally, just as you can pass primitive values to methods or functions, you can likewise pass arrays to systems. Case in point, the accompanying method shows the components in an int array:

```
public static void printarr(int[] arr) {
for (int k = 0; k < arr.length; k++) {
System.out.print(arr[k] + " ");
}
```

You can summon it by passing an array. Case in point, the accompanying declaration conjures the printarr function to show the elements of the array.

```
printarr(new int[]{0, 3, 5, 3, 1});
```

The compilation and execution of this code yields the following result:

0 3 5 3 1

How Can A Method Return An Array

A system might likewise give back an array. Case in point, the method demonstrated underneath returns an array that is the inversion of an alternate array:

```
public static int[] revarr(int[] myarr) {
```

```
int[] resultarr = new int[myarr.length];
for (int k = 0, i = resultarr.length - 1; k <= myarr.length/2; k++, i- -) {
resultarr[j] = myarr[k];
}
return resultarr;
}
```

The Arrays Class

The java.util.arrays class contains different functions for sorting and seeking values from array, looking at arrays, and filling components into arrays. These functions are available for all primitive data types.

- public static boolean equals(long[] a, long[] a2) - returns true if the two indicated arrays are equivalent to each other. Two arrays are viewed as equivalent if both of them contain the same number of components, and all relating sets of components in the two arrays are equivalent. This returns true if the two shows are equivalent. Same function could be utilized by all other primitive data types.
- public static int binarysearch(object[] an, Object key) - looks the pointed out array of Object for the defined value utilizing the double calculation. The array must be sorted before making this call. This returns list of the keys, in the event that it is contained in the list; generally, (-(insertion point + 1).
- public static void sort(Object[] a) – This function can be used to sort a given array in the ascending order. It can likewise be used for any data type.

- public static void fill(int[] an, int val) - appoints the detailed int value to every component of the pointed out array of ints. Same function could be utilized for arrays of other data types as well.

Regular Expressions

Java includes the java.util.regex package to match with regular expressions. Java's normal outflows are fundamentally the same to the Perl programming language and simple to learn. A consistent outflow is an exceptional succession of characters that helps you match or discover different strings or sets of strings, utilizing a specific syntax held as a part of an example. They can be utilized to find, alter, or control content and information. The java.util.regex package essentially comprises of the accompanying three classes:

- Pattern Class: A Pattern article is an arranged representation of a consistent declaration. The Pattern class does not have any public constructors. To make an example, you should first conjure one of its public static methods, which will then give back a Pattern object. These functions acknowledge a normal statement as the first contention.
- Matcher Class: A Matcher article is the motor that translates the example and performs match operations against an information string. Like the Pattern class, Matcher has no public constructors. You get a Matcher object by conjuring the matcher method on a Pattern object.
- Patternsyntaxexception: A Patternsyntaxexception object is an unchecked exemption that shows a sentence structure mistake in a consistent statement design.

Catching Groups

Catching groups are an approach to treat various characters as an issue unit. They are made by putting the characters to be assembled inside a set of enclosures. Case in point, the normal declaration (canine) makes a solitary gathering containing the letters "d", "o", and "g". Catching gatherings are numbered by numbering their opening enclosures from left to right. In the representation ((A)(b(c))), for instance, there are four such gatherings:

- (a)
- (c)
- (b(c))
- ((a)(b(c)))

To discover what number of gatherings are available in the declaration, call the groupcount strategy on a matcher object. The groupcount technique gives back an int demonstrating the quantity of catching gatherings show in the matcher's example. There is likewise an uncommon gathering, gathering 0, which dependably speaks to the whole outflow. This gathering is excluded in the aggregate reported by groupcount.

Sample Implementation:

This sample code emulates how to discover from the given alphanumeric string a digit string:

import java.util.regex.matcher;

import java.util.regex.pattern;

```java
public class Myregexmatches {

public static void primary( String args[] ){

String line = "Request for Qt3000! ";

String example = "(.*)(\\d+)(.*)";

Pattern myr = Pattern.compile(pattern);

Matcher mym = myr.matcher(line);

if (mym.find( )) {

System.out.println("Value = " + mym.group(0) );

System.out.println("Value = " + mym.group(1) );

System.out.println("Value = " + mym.group(2) );

}

else {

System.out.print("No match found!");

}

}
```

Regular Expression Syntax

Given below is a list of regular expression syntax for your reference.

| **Matches** | **Subexpre** |

	ssion
Matches line beginning	^
Matches line end	$
Matches single characters except for the newline character	.
Matches single character in braces	[...]
Matches single character, which are not in braces	[^...]
String beginning	\A
String end	\z
String end except for the final line terminating character	\Z
Matches 0 or more instances of expression	re*
Matches 1 or more instances of the expression	re+
Matches 0 or 1 instances of expression.	re?
Matches exactly n of instances of expression.	re{ n}
Matches n or more instances of the specified expression.	re{ n,}
Matches minimum n and maximum m instances of the expression.	re{ n, m}
Matches one of these: a or b.	a| b
Groups regular expressions. The matching text is remembered.	(re)
Groups regular expressions. The text is not remembered.	(?: re)
Matches independent pattern. No backtracking is supported.	(?> re)
Matches characters in a word.	\w
Matches characters, which are non-word.	\W
Matches whitespace. These characters are equivalent to	\s

[\t\n\r\f].	
Matches space, which is non-whitespace.	\S
Matches digits. These are typically equal to 0 to 9.	\d
Matches non-digits.	\D
Matches string beginning.	\A
Matches string end just before the newline character appears.	\Z
Matches string end.	\z
Matches the point where the last matching condition was found.	\G
Group number n back-reference	\n
Matches boundaries of the word when used without brackets. However, backspace is matched when it is used inside brackets.	\b
Matches boundaries, which are non-word	\B
Matches carriage returns, newlines, and tabs	\n, \t, etc.
Escape all the characters until a \E is found	\Q
Ends any quotes that begin with \Q	\E

Methods of the Matcher Class

Index Methods:

The following table gives a list of methods hat show correctly where the match was found in the info string:

- public int start(int bunch)
  Furnishes a proportional payback record of the subsequent caught by the given group amid the past match operation.

- public int begin()

  Furnishes a proportional payback record of the past match.

- public int end(int bunch)

  Furnishes a proportional payback after the last character of the subsequent caught by the given group amid the past match operation.

- public int end()

  Furnishes a proportional payback after the last character matched.

Study Methods:

Study methods survey the info string and return a Boolean demonstrating whether the example is found:

- public boolean find()

  Endeavors to discover the following subsequence of the info arrangement that matches the example.

- public boolean lookingat()

  Endeavors to match the info arrangement, beginning toward the start of the district, against the example.

- public boolean matches()

  Endeavors to match the whole district against the example.

- public boolean find(int begin)

  Resets this matcher and after that endeavors to discover the following subsequence of the information grouping that matches the example, beginning at the detailed list.

Substitution Methods:

Substitution methods are valuable methods for supplanting content in a data string:

- **public static String quotereplacement(string mystr)**
  Gives back an exacting substitution String for the tagged String. This method creates a String that will function as an issue substitution s in the appendreplacement system for the Matcher class.
- **public Stringbuffer appendtail(stringbuffer strbuff)**
  Actualizes a terminal annex and-supplant step.
- **public Matcher appendreplacement(stringbuffer strbuff, String strsubstitution)**
  Actualizes a non-terminal annex and-supplant step.
- **public String replacefirst(string strsubstitution)**
  Replaces the first subsequence of the data succession that matches the example with the given substitution string.
- **public String replaceall(string strsubstitution)**
  Replaces each subsequence of the data succession that matches the example with the given substitution string.

The begin and end Methods:

Taking after is the sample that tallies the quantity of times the statement "felines" shows up in the data string:

import java.util.regex.pattern;

import java.util.regex.matcher;

public class Regexmatches {

```
private static last String INPUT = "feline cattie feline";

private static last String REGEX = "\\bcat\\b";

public static void principle( String args[] ){

Pattern myp = Pattern.compile(regex);

Matcher mym = myp.matcher(input);

int checkval = 0;

while(mym.find()) {

count++;

System.out.println("match number "+count);

System.out.println("start(): "+mym.start());

System.out.println("end(): "+mym.end());

}

}
```

You can see that this sample uses word limits to guarantee that the letters "c" "a" "t" are not only a substring in a more extended word. It likewise provides for some helpful data about where in the information string the match has happened. The begin technique gives back where its due record of the subsequence caught by the given group amid the past match operation, and end furnishes a proportional payback of the last character matched, in addition to one.

The matches and lookingat Methods:

The matches and lookingat methods both endeavor to match an information succession against an example. The distinction, then again, is that matches requires the whole enter grouping to be matched, while lookingat does not. Both techniques dependably begin toward the start of the data string.

The replacefirst and replaceall Methods:

The replacefirst and replaceall routines supplant content that matches a given standard representation. As their names show, replacefirst replaces the first event, and replaceall replaces all events.

The appendreplacement and appendtail Methods:

The Matcher class additionally gives appendreplacement and appendtail routines to content substitution.

PatternSyntaxException Class Methods:

A PatternSyntaxException is an exception, which is unchecked. This exception indicates a syntactical error in the pattern of the regular expression. The PatternSyntaxException class offers the following methods to the developer for use.

- public int getIndex()
  This function returns the index of error.

- public String getDescription()

  This function returns the description of error.

- public String getMessage()

  This function returns the description and index of error.

- public String getPattern()

  This function returns the error-causing regular expression pattern.

Methods

A Java method is an accumulation of explanations that are gathered together to perform an operation. When you call the System.out.println function, for instance, the framework executes a few articulations so as to show a message on the output screen. Presently, you will figure out how to make your own routines with or without return qualities, call a method with or without parameters, over-loaded methods utilizing the same names, and apply method deliberation in the system plan.

How To Create Methods

Considering the accompanying sample to clarify the structure of a method:

public static int functionname(int x, int y) {

//Statements

}

Here, the method uses the following elements:

- Modifier: public static
- Data type of the return value: int
- Method name: functionname
- Formal Parameters: x, y

Such constructs are otherwise called Functions or Procedures. However, there is a distinctive quality of these two:

- Functions: They return an explicit value.
- Procedures: They don't give back any quality.

Function definition comprises of a system header and body. The construct given above can be generalized to the following arrangement:

modifier returndatatype methodname (List of Parameter) { //Statements }

The structure indicated above incorporates:

- Modifier: It characterizes the right to gain entrance to the method and it is non-compulsory to utilize.
- Returntype: Method may give back a value of this data type.
- Methodname: This is the method name, which comprise of the name and the parameter list of the method.
- List of Parameters: The rundown of parameters, which entails data type, request, and number of parameters of a method. A method may contain zero parameters as well.
- Statements: The method body characterizes what the method does with explanations.

Sample Implementation:

Here is the source code of the above characterized method called maxval(). This technique takes two parameters number1 and number2 and furnishes a proportional payback between the two:

public static int minval(int num1, int num2) {

```
int minvalue;

if (num1 > num2)  minvalue = num2;

else  minvalue = num1;

return minvalue;

}
```

Calling A Method

For utilizing a method, it ought to be called. There are two courses in which a technique is called i.e. technique gives back a value or nothing (no return value). The methodology of system calling is basic. At the point when a project summons a method, the system control gets exchanged to the called method. This called method then returns control to the guest in two conditions. These conditions include:

- Reaches the method closure brace.
- Return articulation is executed.

The methods returning void is considered as call to an announcement. Lets consider a sample:

System.out.println("This is the end of the method!");

The method returning a value can be seen by the accompanying illustration:

double resultant = sumval(4.2, 2.5);

Sample Implementation:

```java
public class Minnumber{

public static void main(string[] args) {

double x = 21.5;

double y = 2.0;

double z = minvalfunc (x, y);

System.out.println("The returned value = " + z);

}

public static double minvalfunc (double num1, double num2) {

double minval;

if (num1 > num2)

minval = num2;

else

minval = num1;

return minval;

}
```

This would create the accompanying result:

The returned value = 2.0

The void Keyword:

The void keyword permits us to make methods, which don't give back a value. Here, in the accompanying illustration we're considering a void method. This function is a void method, which does not give back any value. Call to a void system must be an announcement i.e. rankpoints(657.3);. It is a Java explanation which closes with a semicolon as appeared.

Sample Implementation:

public class Myexample {

public static void main(string[] args) {

rankpoints(657.3);

}

public static void rankpoints(double valfoc) {

if (valfoc >= 100.5) {

System.out.println("A1 Rank");

}

else if (valfoc >= 55.4) {

System.out.println("A2 Rank");

}

else {

System.out.println("A3 Rank");

}

}

This would deliver the accompanying result:

A1 Rank

Passing Parameters by Value

While working under calling procedure, contentions is to be passed. These ought to be in the same request as their particular parameters in the function call. Parameters can be passed by reference or value. Passing parameters by value means calling a method with a parameter. Through, this is the contention value is gone to the parameter.

Sample Implementation:

The accompanying project demonstrates an illustration of passing parameter by value.

public class Myswapping {

public static void main(string[] args) {

double x = 0.43;

double y = 34.65;

System.out.println("Values of X and Y before swapping, x = " + x + " and y = " + y);

```java
myswapfunc (x, y);

System.out.println("\nValues of X and Y after swapping: ");

System.out.println("x = " + x + " and y is " + y);

}

public static void myswapfunc (int x, int y) {

System.out.println("Inside the function: Values of X and Y before swapping, x = " + x + " y = " + y);

System.out.println("Inside the function: Values of X and Y after swapping, x = " + x + " y = " + y);

}
```

Function Overloading

At the point when a class has two or more methods by same name however diverse parameters, it is known as method overloading. It is not the same as overriding. In overriding a method has same name, number of parameters, data type and so on.

The underneath illustration clarifies the same:

```java
public class Myoverloading{

public static void main(string[] args) {

int x = 50;

int y = 34;
```

```java
double s = 14.3;

double r = 13.6;

int resultant1 = minfunc (x, y);

double resultant2 = minfunc (s, r);

System.out.println("Value of minfunc = " + resultant1);

System.out.println("Value of minfunc = " + resultant2);

}

public static int minfunc(int num1, int num2) {

int minval;

if (num1 > num2)

minval = num2;

else

minval = num1;

return minval;

}

public static double minfunc(double num1, double num2) {

double minval;

if (num1 > num2)
```

minval = num2;

else

minval = num1;

return minval;

}

Over-loading systems makes program clear. Here, two systems are given same name yet with distinctive parameters.

Utilizing Command-Line Arguments

Frequently you will need to pass data into a system when you run it. This is expert by passing order line contentions to principle( ). A summon line contention is the data that specifically takes after the program's name on the order line when it is executed. To get to the order line contentions inside a Java system is truly easy.they are put away as strings in the String cluster went to fundamental( ).

Sample Implementation:

public class Mycommandline {

public static void main(string args[]){

for(int k=0; k<args.length; k++){

System.out.println("ARGS[" + k + "]: " + args[k]);

}

}

The Constructors:

A constructor instates an item when it is made. It has the same name as its class and is linguistically like a system. On the other hand, constructors have no return data type. Regularly, you will utilize a constructor to give beginning values to the instance variables characterized by the class, or to perform whatever other startup methods are needed to make a completely structured item.

All classes have constructors, whether you characterize one or not, on the grounds that Java naturally gives a default constructor that instates all variables to zero. Then again, once you characterize your own constructor, the default constructor is no more utilized.

Sample Implementation:

class Myconsclass {

int i;

Myconsclass() {

i = 0;

}

You would call constructor to introduce objects as shown below:

public class Myconsdemo {

public static void main(string args[]) {

```
Myconsclass tcons1 = new Myconsclass ();

Myconsclass tcons2 = new Myconsclass ();

System.out.println(tcons1.i + " + tcons2.i);

}
```

Regularly, you will require a constructor that acknowledges one or more parameters. Parameters are added to a constructor in the same way that they are added to a strategy, simply declare them inside the brackets after the constructor's name.

Sample Implementation:

```
class MyNewclass {

int x;

MyNewclass(int k ) {

x = k;

}
```

You would call constructor to introduce objects in the manner shown below:

```
public class Myconsdemo {

public static void main(string args[]) {

Myconsclass tcons1 = new Myclass( 35 );
```

Myconsclass tcons2 = new Myclass(67);

System.out.println(tcons1.x + " "+ tcons2.x);

}

This would create the accompanying result:

35 67

Variable Arguments(var-args)

Java Development Kit 1.5 empowers you to pass arguments, which can be of variable number. However, the data type of the parameters should be the same. The parameter in the system is declared in the following manner:

typename... nameofparameter

In the statement, you define the data type emulated by an ellipsis (...). Only one variable-length parameter may be determined in a method, and this parameter must be the last parameter. Any customary parameters must go before it.

Sample Implementation:

public class Mysampleclass {

public static void main(string args[]) {

printmaxval(33, 45, 43, 22, 5);

printmaxval(new double[]{5, 8, 1});

}

```java
public static void printmaxval( double... mynum) {

if (mynum.length == 0) {

System.out.println("No Arguments!");

return;

}

double resultant = mynum [0];

for (int x = 1; x < mynum.length; x++)

if (mynum[x] > resultant)  resultant = mynum[x];

System.out.println("Max val = " + resultant); }
```

This would deliver the accompanying result:

Max val = 45.0

Max val = 1.0

The finalize( ) Method:

It is conceivable to call a method that will be called just before an object's last annihilation. This method is referred to as finalize(), and it can be utilized to guarantee that an item ends neatly. For instance, you may utilize finalize( ) to verify that an open record possessed by that object is shut. To add a finalizer to a class, you basically jus call finalize(). The Java runtime calls that technique at whatever point it is going to reuse an object of that class.

Inside this function, you will point out those activities that must be performed before an object is removed. The syntax of using and implementing this function is:

protected void finalize( ) {

//Statements

}

The access modifier used for the method ensures that the method cannot be accessed by elements outside the particular class. This implies that you can't know when or how the method executes.

File Handling

All the classes that you may require on a day to day I/O programming basis are contained in the package java.io. The streams present in this package broadly represent output and input locations. Moreover, the streams supported in Java include object, primitives and localized characters. A stream can simply be described as data, arranged in a sequence. While the inputStream can be used for inputting data from a source, the OutputStream can be sued for outputting data to a sink. The support for I/O provided by Java is flexible and extensive. This chapter sims to cover all the basic facets of File Handling in Java.

Byte Streams

Byte streams in Java are utilized to perform output and input of 8-bit bytes. In spite of the fact that there are numerous classes identified with byte streams yet most utilized classes are, Fileoutputstream and Fileinputstream. Here is an example of they can be used in real-life programming.

```
import java.io.*;
public class Filecopy {
public static void main(string args[]) throws IOException {
FileInputStream inputx = invalid;
FileOutputStream outputx = invalid;
try {
inputx = new FileInputStream("inputfile.txt");
outputx = new FileOutputStream("outputfile.txt");
int charx;
while ((charx = inputx.read()) != -1) {
```

```
outputx.write(charx);
}
}
finally {
if (inputx != invalid) {
inputx.close();
}
if (outputx != invalid) {
outputx.close();
}
}
}
```

Presently we should have a record inputfile.txt with the accompanying content:

This is for testing purpose only.

As an important step, compile and execute the code shown above. The execution of the code shall result in the creation of outputfile.txt file.

Character Streams

Java Byte streams are utilized to perform output and input of 8-bit bytes. On the other hand, Java Character streams are utilized to perform output and input for 16-bit unicode. In spite of the fact that there are numerous classes identified with character streams yet the most commonly used ones include Filereader and Filewriter.

It is worth mentioning here that the implementation of Filereader utilizes Fileinputstream and Filewriter utilizes Fileoutputstream. This may make you wonder as to what is the difference between the former and latter. Filereader peruses two bytes at once and Filewriter composes two bytes at once. We can re-compose above sample which makes utilization of these two classes to duplicate an info record (having unicode characters) into an outputfile.txt.

```java
import java.io.*;
public class Mycopyfile {
public static void main(string args[]) throws IOException {
FileReader inputx = invalid;
FileWriter outputx = invalid;
try {
inputx = new FileReader("inputfile.txt");
outputx = new FileWriter("outputfile.txt");
int charx;
while ((charx = inputx.read()) != -1) {
outputx.write(charx);
}
}
finally {
if (inputx != invalid) {
inputx.close();
}
if (outputx != invalid) {
outputx.close();
}
}
}
}
```

Presently how about we have a record inputfile.txt with the accompanying text:

This is for testing purpose only.

Compile and execute the file containing this code. The execution of this code should create an output file outputfile.txt.

Standard Streams

All the programming languages give backing to standard I/O where client's code can take information from a console and afterward deliver appropriate output on the machine screen. On the off chance that you have some knowledge of C or C++, then you must be mindful of three standard tools namely, STDIN, STDOUT and STDERR. Java provides three standard streams, which are discussed below:

- Standard Error: This is utilized to yield the error information created by the client's code and normally a machine screen is utilized as standard error stream and referred to as System.err.
- Standard Output: This is utilized to yield the information created by the client's code and normally a machine screen is utilized to standard output stream and referred to as System.out.
- Standard Input: This is utilized to encourage the information to client's code and normally a console is utilized as standard data stream and referred to as System.in.

Sample Implementation:

```
import java.io.*;
public class Myreadconsole {
public static void main(string args[]) throws IOException {
InputStreamReader cinx = invalid;
try {
cinx = new InputStreamReader(system.in);
```

```java
System.out.println("Input string, press "e" to exit.");
char charx;
do {
charx = (char) cinx.read();
System.out.print(charx);
} while(charx != 'e');
}
finally {
if (cinx != invalid) {
cinx.close();
}
}
}
```

The code mentioned above must be saved in a file named Myreadconsole.java. Upon compilation and execution of this code, the system must be able to receive and interpret characters.

Perusing and Writing Files

As mentioned previously, a stream can be defined as a sequence of information. The Inputstream is utilized to peruse information from a source and the Outputstream is utilized for outputting information to a terminus.

Here is a chain of importance of classes to manage Input and Output streams. The two essential streams are Fileinputstream and Fileoutputstream, which would be talked about in the following section:

Fileinputstream:

This stream is utilized for perusing information from the documents. Objects can be made utilizing the keyword new and there are a few sorts of constructors accessible. Inputstream can be used for reading files in the following manner:

Inputstream myfx = new Fileinputstream("c:/java/hi");

The constructor takes a record item to make a data stream object to peruse the document. Initially, we make a record item utilizing File() technique in the following manner:

File myfx = new File("c:/java/hi");

Inputstream myfx = new Fileinputstream(myfx);

When you have the object of Inputstream under control, there is a rundown of assistant methods, which can be utilized to peruse to stream or to do different operations on the stream.

- protected void finalize() throws IOException {}
  This system cleans up any association with the file and guarantees that the local method for this output stream for the file is called. Besides this, this method is also capable of throwing an exception.
- public void close() throws IOException {}
  This system shuts the output stream of the file and discharges any framework assets connected with the the same. It is also capable of throwing an exception.
- public int available() throws IOException{}
  This function returns an int, indicating the number of bytes that the input stream can still read.
- public int read(int r)throws IOException{}

The read method is used for reading content from the InputStream and returns the next byte of data in int data type. However, upon reaching the end of file, it returns -1.
- public int read(byte[] r) throws IOException{}
  This read method is similar in operation to the read method described above with the exception that it reads data length of r in the given array. The function returns the number of bytes read and -1 upon reaching the end of file.

Other input streams are also available for use. Some of these include:

- DataInputStream
- ByteArrayInputStream

FileOutputStream:

Fileoutputstream is utilized to make a file and write text into it. The stream would create a file, in the event that it doesn't as of now exist, before opening it for outputting. Here are two constructors which can be utilized to make a Fileoutputstream object.

Method 1:

OutputStream myfx = new FileOutputStream("c:/java/hi")

Method 2:

File myfx = new File("c:/java/hi");

OutputStream myfx = new FileOutputStream(myfx);

When you have OutputStream object under control, there is a rundown of aide methods, which can be utilized to keep in touch with stream or to do different operations on the stream.

- public void write(int w) throws IOException {}
  This method composes the tagged byte to the output stream.
- protected void finalize() throws IOException {}
  This strategy cleans up any associations with the record. Besides this, it also guarantees that the local method for this output stream for file is called. This method is capable of throwing an exception.
- public void close() throws IOException {}
  This method shuts the output stream of the file. Moreover, it discharges any framework assets connected with the document. This method also throws an IOException.
- public void write(byte[] w)
  This method composes w.length bytes from the specified byte exhibit to the Outputstream.

There are other imperative output streams accessible, which are as follows:

- ByteArrayOutputStream
- DataOutputStream

Sample Implementations:

import java.io.*;

public class Mytestfile{

```java
public static void main(string args[]){

try{

byte bytewrite [] = {45,64,22,49,1};

OutputStream myos = new FileOutputStream("mytest.txt");

for(int i=0; i < bytewrite.length ; i++){

myos.write( bytewrite[x] );

}

myos.close();

InputStream myis = new FileInputStream("mytest.txt");

int sizex = myis.available();

for(int z=0; z< sizex; z++){

System.out.print((char)myis.read() + " ");

}

myis.close();

}catch(IOException e){

System.out.print("Exception Caught!");

}

}
```

The above code would make a file mytest.txt and would compose given numbers in parallel organization. Same would be outputted to the stdout screen.

File Navigation and I/O

There are a few different classes that we would be experiencing to get to know the fundamentals of File Navigation and I/O.

- File Class
- FileWriter Class
- FileReader Class

Directories

A directory is a File, which can contains a rundown of different catalogs and files. You utilize the object File to make catalogs, to rundown down documents accessible in an index. For complete point of interest check a rundown of every last one of techniques which you can approach File item and what are identified with indexes.

Making Directories:

There are two valuable File utility methods, which can be utilized to make directories:

- The mkdirs() method makes both a directory and all the elements of the index.
- The mkdir( ) method makes a directory, returning valid on achievement and false on disappointment. Failure demonstrates that the way determined in the File object exists,

or that the index can't be made in light of the fact that the whole way does not exist yet.

Sample Implementation:

```java
import java.io.File;
public class MyCreateDir {
public static void main(String args[]) {
String directoryname = "/tmp/user/java/bin";
File dir = new File(directoryname);
dir.mkdirs();
}
}
```

Listing Directories:

You can utilize list( ) method provided by the File class to provide a list of all the records and directories accessible in an index.

Sample Implementation:

```java
import java.io.File;
public class MyReadDir {
public static void main(String[] args) {
File myfile = null;
String[] paths;
try{
myfile = new File("/tmp");
mypaths = file.list();
for(String path:mypaths)
{
```

```
            System.out.println(path);
        }
    }catch(Exception e){
        e.printStackTrace();
    }
    }
}
```

Exception Handling

During the execution of your program, it may experience abnormal or exceptional conditions. As a result of these, the system may crash. An exception may occur due to a number of reasons. Some of these include:

- A file that needs to be opened can't be found.
- A client has entered invalid information.
- A system association has been lost amidst correspondences or the JVM has used up all the available memory.

Some of these special cases are created by client mistake, others by developer blunder, and others by physical assets that have fizzled into your code in some way. To see how exception handling works in Java, you have to comprehend the three classifications of exceptions:

- Errors: These are not special cases whatsoever. Therefore, errors can be defined as issues that are beyond the understanding and the ability to control of the client or the software engineer. They are normally overlooked in your code on the grounds that you can once in a while take care of a mistake. Case in point, if a stack overflow happens, it is sure to result in an error. They are additionally disregarded at the time of compiling.
- Runtime Exceptions: It is a special case that most likely could have been dodged by the software engineer. Runtime exceptions are disregarded at the time of assemblage.

- Checked Exceptions: It is a special case that is regularly a client mistake or an issue that can't be predicted by the developer. Case in point, if a file is to be opened, yet the file can't be found, an exception of this type happens. These special cases can't just be disregarded at the time of compilation and dry runs.

Hierarchy of Exceptions

All classes of exceptions are subtypes of the java.lang.exception class. This class is a subclass of the Throwable class. Other than the exception class, there is an alternate subclass called Error which is gotten from the Throwable class. These special case scenarios are not ordinarily caught by the Java programs. These conditions ordinarily happen if alternate scenarios are not taken care of by the java programs. Errors are produced to demonstrate lapses created by the runtime environment. A sample exception is: Out of Memory or Stack Overflow. The Exception class has two primary subclasses: IOException and RuntimeException Classes.

Exception Methods:

Here is a list of methods that are available as part of the Throwable class.

- public Throwable getcause()
  This method gives back the cause of the exemption as mentioned by a Throwable item.
- public String getmessage()

This method gives back the exception's complete message and details. This message is usually included in the Throwable constructor.

- public void printstacktrace()

    This method prints the aftereffect of tostring() alongside the stack follow to System.err, the output stream for error.

- public String tostring()

    The method gives back where its due of the class linked with the aftereffect of getmessage()

- public Throwable fillinstacktrace()

    The method fills the stack of this Throwable object with the current trace of stack, adding to any past data in the trace of stack.

- public Stacktraceelement [] getstacktrace()

    The method gives back a array containing every component on the trace of stack. The component at file o speaks to the highest point of the call stack, and the last component in the show speaks to the system at the base of the call stack.

Getting Exceptions:

A system discovers a special case utilizing a blend of the try and catch keywords. A try scope is set around the code that may produce an exemption. Code inside this scope is alluded to as secured code, and the structure for utilizing try/catch is given below:

try {

//Code that may produce an exception

}catch(nameofexception exp_1) {

//Code to be executed once an exception occurs

}

A try block includes announcing the kind of exception you are attempting to get. In the event that an exception happens in ensured code, the catch square that executes after the attempt is checked. In the event that this sort of special case that happened in a try block, the exception goes to the catch block, which is also passed as a system parameter.

Sample Implementation:

import java.io.*;

public class MyException{

public static void main(string args[]){

try{

int myarr[] = new int[2];

System.out.println("This statement attempts to access the third element of the array:" + a[3]);

}catch(arrayindexoutofboundsexception e_1){

System.out.println("The thrown exception is: " + e_1);

}

System.out.println("Exception: Out of Bounds");

}

This would deliver the accompanying result:

The thrown exception is: java.lang.arrayindexoutofboundsexception: 3

Exception: Out of Bounds

Using Multiple Try Blocks

A single piece of code can have a number of catch blocks for catching different exceptions. The structure of the multiple try/catch blocks is given below:

try {

//Statements to be tested

}catch(exceptiontype1 e_1) {

//Catch block 1

}

catch(exceptiontype2 e_2) {

//Catch block 2

}catch(exceptiontype3 e_3) {

//Catch block 3

}

This code uses three catches. However, you can use as many catch blocks as you need for your code. On the off chance that an exception happens in the protected code, the exemption is thrown and caught firstly by the first catch block. If the exception type matches, then the catch block executes. However, if the exception type doesn't match, the exception is open to be caught by the next catch block. This process continues until a matching exception type is found or all the catch blocks have been checked.

Sample Implementation:

try{

filex = new Fileinputstream(nameoffile);

num = (byte) filex.read();

}catch(IOException e_1) {

e_1.printstacktrace();

return -1;

}catch(filenotfoundexception f_1){

f_1.printstacktrace();

return -1;

}

Throws Keyword

On the off chance that a system does not handle a checked exception, the method must proclaim it utilizing the keyword throws. The throws keyword shows up toward the end of a the method's signature. You can throw an exemption, either a recently instantiated one or a special case that you simply found, by utilizing the keyword throw.

Finally Keyword

The keyword finally is utilized to make a piece of code that last code to be executed for a program. A finally square of code dependably executes, irrespective of whether an exemption has happened or not. Utilizing a finally piece permits you to run any cleanup-sort statements that you need to execute, regardless of what happens in the secured code.

Creating An Exception

You can make your own exemptions in Java. Remember the accompanying focuses when composing your classes for exceptions:

- All exemptions must be an offspring of Throwable.
- If you need to compose a checked exemption that is naturally authorized by the Handle or Declare Rule, you have to create an extension of the Exception class.
- If you need to compose a runtime exemption, you will have to create an extension of the Runtimeexception class.

You can create your own exceptions using the following structure:

class MyNewException extends Exception{ }

Common Exceptions

In Java, it is conceivable to characterize two categories of Exceptions and Errors.

- Programmatic exceptions: - These special cases are tossed unequivocally by the application or the API software engineers Examples: Illegalargumentexception, IllegalStateException.
- JVM Exceptions: - These are exemptions/mistakes that are solely or consistently thrown by the JVM. Some exceptions of this class are ArrayIndexOutOfBoundsException, NullPointerException and ClassCastException.

Interfaces and Packages

Abstract methods when brought together form a package. A class actualizes an interface, consequently inheriting the interface's abstract methods. An interface is not a class. Composing an interface is like composing a class. However, they are two separate ideas. A class portrays the properties and behaviours of an object. On the other hand, An interface contains behaviours that a class shall implement.

Unless the class that actualizes the interface is abstract, all the methods for the interface need to be implemented in the class. An interface is like a class in the accompanying ways:

- An interface is composed in a file with a .java augmentation, with the name of the interface matching the name of the file.
- An interface can contain any number of methods.
- Interfaces show up in packages, and their relating bytecode file must be in a directory structure that matches the name of the package.
- The bytecode of an interface shows up in a .class record.

On the other hand, an interface is unique and different from a class in a few ways. These are:

- An interface does not contain any constructors.
- Interface cannot be instantiated

- Instance fields cannot be contained in an interface. It is a requirement of interfaces that the main fields in them must be final and static.
- It is a requirement that all of the methods must be abstract methods.
- An interface can extend different interfaces.
- A class does not access an interface. Actually, a class implements an interface.

Declaring Interfaces

In order to declare an interface, you must use the interface keyword. Here is a straightforward illustration that can be used for declaring an interface. The standard structure and order of statements that can be used for this purpose are as follows:

import java.lang.*;

public interface Interfacename {

//Statements

}

Interfaces have the accompanying properties:

- An interface is verifiably dynamic. You don't have to utilize the keyword abstract when declaring an interface.
- Each method in an interface is additionally dynamic, so the keyword abstract is not required.
- Methods in an interface are certainly public.

Sample Implementation

interface MyAnimal {

public void eatinghabits();

public void walkinghabits();

}

Packages

Packages are utilized as a part of Java so as to avert naming clashes, to control access, to make seeking/placing and utilization of classes, interfaces, identifications and annotations less demanding, in addition to several others. A Package can be described as a collection of related types (classes, interfaces, counts and annotations) giving access security and name space administration.

A few packages available in Java are::

- java.io – all the classes for output and input are available in this package
- java.lang – all the major classes are available in this package

Developers can create their own packages or package collections of classes/interfaces, and so on. It is a decent practice to collect related classes executed by you so that a software engineer can undoubtedly discover that the interfaces, classes, annotations and counts can be connected. Since the package makes another namespace, there won't be any name clashes with names in different packages. Utilizing packages, it is less demanding to give access control and it is likewise simpler to find the related classes.

At the point when you create a package, you ought to pick a name and put a explanation with that name at the highest point of each source record that contains the classes, interfaces, lists, and annotation sorts that you need to incorporate in the package. The package declaration ought to be the first line in the source record. There can be one and only declaration in each one source record, and it applies to various sorts in the file. In the event that a declaration of interface is not utilized, then the interfaces, class, annotation and specifications will be put in a package, which will be unnamed.

Java Applets

In order to run an applet, you must have a web browser. An applet can be a completely utilitarian Java application on the grounds that it has the whole Java API's available to it. There are some essential contrasts between an applet and a standalone Java application, including the accompanying:

- A main() function is not conjured on an applet, and an applet class won't define main().
- An applet is a Java class that extends and enhances the java.applet.applet class.
- When a client sees a HTML page that contains an applet, the code for the applet is automatically downloaded to the client's machine.
- Applets are intended to be inserted inside a HTML page.
- The JVM on the client's machine makes an instance of the applet class and conjures different routines amid the applet's lifetime.
- The security requirements for an applets are very strict. The security of an applet is frequently alluded to as sandbox security, contrasting the applet with a youngster playing in a sandbox with different decides that must be emulated.
- A JVM is a base requirement for viewing an applet. The JVM can be either a module of the Web program or a different runtime environment.
- Other classes that the applet needs can be downloaded in a solitary Java Archive (JAR) file.

Life Cycle of an Applet

The creation of any applet requires the implementation of four methods of the Applet class. These methods have been discussed in the text below.

- init: This method is planned for whatever introduction is required for your applet. It is called after the param labels inside the applet tag have been transformed.
- start: This method is naturally called after the program calls the init strategy. It is likewise called at whatever point the client comes back to the page containing the applet in the wake of having gone off to different pages.
- stop: This method is consequently called when the client leaves the page on which the applet sits. It can, accordingly, be called over and over in the same applet.
- destroy: This technique is just called when the program closes down. Since applets are intended to live on a HTML page, you ought not regularly desert assets after a client leaves the page that contains the applet.
- paint: This method is invoked quickly after the start() method. Furthermore, whenever the applet needs to repaint itself in the program, this method needs to be called. The paint() method is inherited from the java.awt.

A "Welcome, World" Applet

The accompanying is a basic applet named BasicApplet.java:

```
import java.applet.*;

import java.awt.*;

public class BasicApplet extends Applet {

public void paint (Graphics gx)  {

gx.drawstring ("Say Hello To The World!", 35, 70);

}
```

These import explanations bring the classes into the extent of our applet class:

- java.awt.graphics
- java.applet.applet

Without those import explanations, the Java compiler would not perceive the classes Applet and Graphics, which the applet class alludes to.

The Applet Class

Each applet is an augmentation of the java.applet.applet class. The base Applet class gives techniques that a determined Applet class may call to get data and administrations from the program connection. These incorporate techniques that do the accompanying:

- Get parameters of the applet
- Get the system area of the HTML record that contains the applet

- Get the system area of the applet class registry
- Print a status message in the program
- Fetch a picture
- Fetch a sound
- Play a sound
- Perform resizing of the applet

Moreover, the Applet class gives an interface by which the viewer or program gets data about the applet and controls the applet's execution. The viewer might:

- Request data about the form, creator and copyright of the applet
- Request a depiction of the parameters the applet perceives
- Perform applet initialization
- Perform applet destruction
- Begin the execution of the applet
- Stop the execution of the applet

The Applet class allows default usage of each of these routines. Those executions may be overridden as essential. The "Say Hello To The World!" applet is complete in itself. However, as part of the implementation, only the paint() function is over-ridden.

Other Scott Sanderson Books:

jQuery, JavaScript, and HTML5: A Simple Start to jQuery, JavaScript, and HTML5 (Written by a Software Engineer)

C++ Programming For Beginners: A Simple Start To C++ Programming Written By A Software Engineer

PHP Programming and MySQL For Beginners: A Simple Start To PHP & MySQL Written By A Software Engineer

BONUS: Free Books & Special Offers
I want to thank you again for reading this book! I would like to give you access to a great service that will e-mail you notifications when we have FREE books available. You will have FREE access to some great titles before they get marked at the normal retail price that everyone else will pay. This is a no strings attached offer simply for being a great customer.

*Simply go to www.globalizedhealing.com to get free books.

Copyright 2014 by Globalized Healing, LLC - All rights reserved.

Printed in Great Britain
by Amazon.co.uk, Ltd.,
Marston Gate.